RESTYLING JUNK

To Bryan, Kate, Toby and Beth
with love

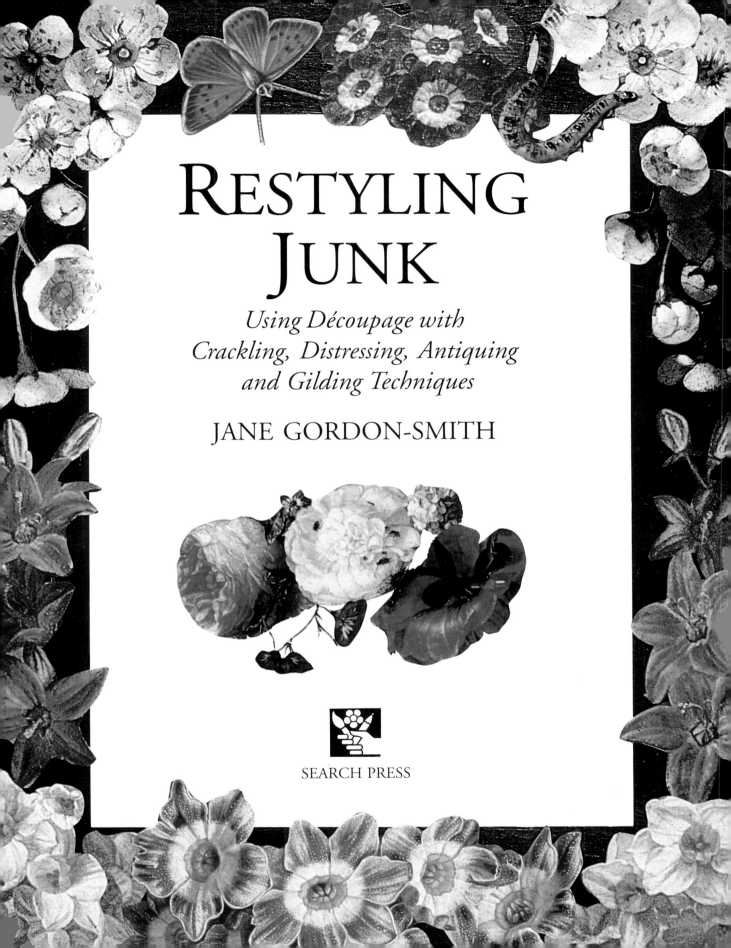

RESTYLING JUNK

*Using Découpage with
Crackling, Distressing, Antiquing
and Gilding Techniques*

JANE GORDON-SMITH

SEARCH PRESS

First published in Great Britain 1998

Search Press Limited
Wellwood, North Farm Road,
Tunbridge Wells, Kent TN2 3DR

ISBN 0 85532 863 0

Suppliers
If you have any difficulty in obtaining any of the
materials and equipment mentioned in this book,
then please write for a current list of stockists,
including firms who operate a mail-order service, to
the Publishers:

Search Press Limited, Wellwood,
North Farm Road, Tunbridge Wells,
Kent TN2 3DR, England

Publishers' note
Always follow the manufacturer's instructions
when using oil- or spirit-based products. Use in a
well-ventilated room and keep away from children.

The Publishers would like to thank National Gallery
Publications Limited, Trafalgar Square, London WC2N
5DN; Mamelok Press Limited, Northern Way, Bury St
Edmunds, Suffolk, IP32 6NJ; and Woodmansterne
Publications Limited, 1 The Boulevard, Blackmoor Lane,
Watford, Hertfordshire, WD1 8YW for their kind
permission to use the giftwrap images featured in this book.

With thanks also to Fenwick Limited, Royal Victoria
Place, Tunbridge Wells, Kent TN1 2SR for loaning the
pillows, pillow cases and duvet cover featured on pages 28–
29 and on the front cover.

Printed in Spain by Elkar S. Coop. Bilbao 48012

OPPOSITE
*This mirror has been gilded with aluminium leaf and
decorated with pale blue colourwashed prints. Three
coats of shellac were then applied, to give a rich gold
colouring. The candlesticks were découpaged using a
black and white print coloured with French polish.*

Contents

INTRODUCTION

I was married in 1970 and started painting furniture at that time. In those days, we had little money and so the restyling of my junk shop finds was a necessity. My husband's job then took him to many different countries and the children and I went too. Being abroad gave me the opportunity to experiment with a variety of styles of painted and decorated furniture and I soon became aware of many differences. What was popular in the temperate climate of Britain was not necessarily in vogue in other parts of Europe, Australia or Singapore.

I always think of Sweden as being the home of painted furniture, and it has certainly been popular there for a long time. I believe that it was the Swedish artist Karl Larson and his wife Karin who first introduced the technique of painting furniture one hundred years ago. Their influence has lasted to this day, but they began for the same reason that I did in 1970 – lack of money!

My introduction to découpage came later. We finally settled back in Britain in 1987 and at the same time the National Gallery printed a gift wrap collection featuring some of their Dutch flower paintings. I felt that these gift wraps were too beautiful to use merely for wrapping up presents, and so I started cutting them out and sticking the cut-out images on to bed heads. My enthusiasm for this technique soon grew, and I decided to start up a

business. I now sell painted and découpaged furniture and accessories to the trade and I export to many countries, including Norway, Italy and the USA. I also teach at various art centres around the country.

I have divided this book roughly into chronological chapters which show the different styles of decorated furniture through the years. There is a section at the beginning showing all the basic techniques, including how to apply découpage, use crackle varnish, distress a surface and gild using Dutch metal leaf. There are easy to follow step-by-step instructions with lots of photographs, and the projects cover working on different surfaces such as wood, metal, china, glass and cardboard. I have also included a section at the back to help you put things right if you go wrong.

I hope this book will inspire you to go out and find your own objects to restyle. Try scouring your local junk shop or go to a car boot sale. Do not be put off by the colour or decoration of an object – concentrate on the shape. You should also try to choose objects that are well-made and need as little work in preparation as possible. Filling in holes and treating for woodworm can be very tedious and time-consuming.

You do not have to be an expert artist to be competent at découpage; you just need to learn how best to use other artists' masterpieces to create your own style. Most importantly, use your imagination and have fun!

MATERIALS

Listed below are the materials used for the paint effects, découpage and gilding shown in this book. They are all available from art and craft shops or hardware stores, and most newsagents stock gift wrap.

The materials required for each project are listed. In addition, you will need paper towelling for general mopping up, and white spirit and/or methylated spirit for cleaning brushes after use.

1. Water-based paints

Water-based emulsion paint can be used on most materials.

2. Artist's oil paints

Oil paint is used to show up the cracks when using the crackling technique. Burnt or raw Sienna or umber are the traditional colours used, but any coloured oil paint will work.

3. Watercolour paints

These are used to colour black and white photocopies.

4. Découpage paper and scraps

There is a huge selection of gift wrap available. Thin paper is better than thick. You can also buy images specially designed for découpage. Coloured or black and white photocopies are useful, particularly if you do not want to use an original piece such as a photograph.

5. Scissors

Small, sharp, pointed scissors are essential. I use straight-bladed scissors but some people find curved ones easier.

6. Brushes

Buy good quality varnish brushes and keep them exclusively for varnish. You will need one for water-based, one for oil-based and one for spirit-based varnish. You will also need a brush for paint and one for glue. The size of your brushes depends on the object to be decorated.

7. Chalk

Chalk is useful for marking the position of your design before gluing it in place.

8. Craft knife or scalpel

You can use a craft knife or scalpel for cutting out images, but I prefer to use scissors. A craft knife or scalpel is useful for cutting through a design to enable a box lid to open, for example, or to divide the panels of a screen. It is also used to remove bubbles under paper (see page 62).

9. Candle wax

This is used during the distressing technique, to artificially age a surface.

10. Metal primer

A commercial primer is available, designed for use specifically on metal.

11. Water-based gold size

A water-based gold size is used for sticking Dutch metal leaf on to a surface.

12. Methylated spirit

Brushes used with spirit-based products can be cleaned with methylated spirit.

13. White spirit

Brushes used with oil-based products can be cleaned with white spirit.

14. Sticky plastic (removable adhesive)

You will find sticky plastic useful for holding cut-outs in place on vertical objects prior to gluing them.

15. Wax polish

This is used for polishing a finished surface.

16. Gold, aluminium and copper Dutch metal leaf

These are used for gilding.

17. Metallic paints
Metallic paints can be used to fill in any small cracks that are left after gilding.

18. Wire wool
Very fine wire wool is used to apply wax polish. It can also be used to remove rust.

19. Duster
You will need a duster for polishing.

20. Cloth
A damp cloth is used to remove residue after sanding.

21. Paper towelling
Paper towelling is used to apply oil paint and for general mopping up.

22. Sandpaper
Use fine wet-and-dry sandpaper to rub down varnish in between coats. Medium and coarse grade sandpaper will be needed to prepare surfaces for painting and for distressing paint.

23. PVA Glue
PVA glue is suitable for découpage. For all projects in this book, a mixture of PVA glue and water should be used unless otherwise stated. The PVA glue should be diluted until it is the consistency of thin cream.

24. Sanding sealer
This is a clear spirit-based lacquer used for sealing crackle varnish. It can also be used in place of shellac, although it is clear in colour.

25. Oil-based varnish
Oil-based varnish is used after crackling and also if a really tough or heat-resistant finish is needed.

26. Water-based varnish
Use a quick-drying water-based acrylic varnish. This is readily available in hardware shops.

27. Shellac
Shellac is a spirit-based honey-coloured lacquer that is used for antiquing. French polish, white polish and knotting all belong to the same spirit-based family and can be used in place of shellac, although they all differ in colour. Sanding sealer can also be used, but it is clear-drying.

Shellac can be used to prime wood or cardboard. Commercial primers designed for use on specific materials are also available.

28. Crackle varnish
Two bottles of specialist varnish which together produce a crackled finish are available from art and craft shops. There are many different types, so read the instructions carefully. I use two-hour gold size as the undercoat and gum arabic solution as the top coat. The instructions for using these are shown on page 17.

29. Sponge
A damp sponge is useful when gluing.

30. Hairdryer
The crackling process involves the use of heat, and a hairdryer is ideal for this purpose.

1. Water-based paints

10. Metal primer

These are the basic materials required for applying découpage with various decorative finishes. For information about these materials, refer to pages 8–9.

2. Artist's oil paints

3. Watercolour paints

5. Scissors

4. Découpage paper and scraps

7. Chalk

8. Craft knife or scalpel

6. Brushes

9. Candle wax

12. *Methylated spirit*

15. *Wax polish*

14. *Sticky plastic*

22. *Sandpaper*

11. *Water-based gold size*

21. *Paper towelling*

13. *White spirit*

20. *Cloth*

16. *Gold, aluminium and copper Dutch metal leaf*

18. *Wire wool*

19. *Duster*

17. *Metallic paints*

24. *Sanding sealer*

29. *Sponge*

27. *Shellac*

23. *PVA glue*

26. *Water-based varnish*

30. *Hairdryer*

25. *Oil-based varnish*

28. *Crackle varnish*

TECHNIQUES

Basic techniques

This section covers the basic techniques used in this book. The projects are all based on découpage which is not a difficult craft as it essentially involves just cutting out images, arranging a design and then gluing it in place. These techniques, although simple, do require time and patience. Careful cutting out is particularly important as it can make all the difference to a finished piece.

Cutting out

Cut around the image using a pair of small, sharp, pointed scissors. Move the paper and not the scissors. Make sure you cut away all the background, including any 'islands' of background in the middle of your design. To do this, pierce into the centre of the island with the tip of the scissors and then snip around it. If there are a lot of islands cut them out first, before the paper gets too flimsy.

Arranging a design

Move the paper cut-outs around until you are happy with the design. Pay attention to the shadows and do not put dark areas over light ones. Check that all the details are correct, for example that dew drops are dripping downwards and that insects are flying the right way up. When you are happy with the arrangement, glue in place with diluted PVA glue.

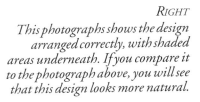

ABOVE
This photograph shows the wrong way to arrange a design. Notice how placing dark areas of images on top of light areas, creates an unnatural-looking design.

NOTE

If you are working on a perpendicular surface, use sticky plastic to hold the cut-out elements in place. They can then be moved around until you are happy with your design.

Do not forget to remove the sticky plastic from the back of the cut-outs before gluing in place.

RIGHT
This photographs shows the design arranged correctly, with shaded areas underneath. If you compare it to the photograph above, you will see that this design looks more natural.

Working on a spherical surface

2. Stick the design on to a glass sphere using diluted PVA glue. Try to overlap the cuts to produce a natural-looking image.

1. Snip into the design at several points so that the paper will overlap itself when glued on to a spherical object. Always cut with the design. For example, if you are working on a flower, cut around petals.

---- NOTE ----

You can stick a design on to the outside of a glass container, or on to the inside (see page 57), depending on whether you want a functional or purely decorative piece.

Colouring a design

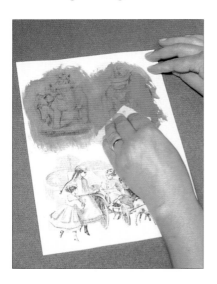

To colourwash a black and white photocopy, thin your paint with a little water. Choose a colour to complement the surface that it will be stuck on to. Brush the paint on quickly, and then immediately wipe it off with a damp sponge or some paper towelling. The image will now show through but the background will be coloured. When stuck on to a surface, the colourwashed design will look as if it has been drawn directly on.

---- NOTE ----

As an alternative to colourwashing, a black and white print can be painted with watercolour paints or pencils (see page 24).

An antique finish can be achieved by brushing on a thin coat of shellac over a coloured design (see the magazine rack on page 36).

Making a straight border

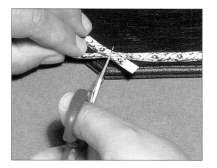

2. Where the borders cross at the corners, cut both pieces through the centre of the cross. Glue in place using diluted PVA glue.

1. Cut the border into strips roughly the same length as each edge, allowing for a small overlap. Place the strips on the object, with the corners overlapping. Paste the centre of each strip down using diluted PVA glue. Do not glue down the ends of each border strip.

Making a curved border

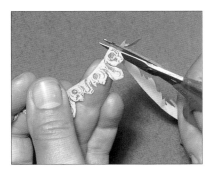

1. Make cuts into the border strips to enable them to be eased around a curve. Cut with the design, and snip almost up to the outside edge.

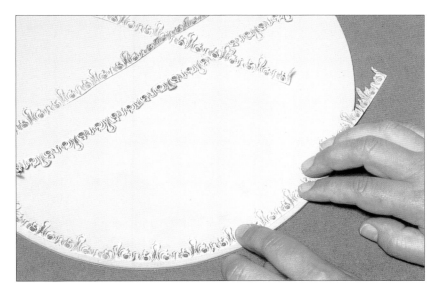

2. Paste the back of each strip with diluted PVA glue. Place the border on to your object. Ease it into position so that the cuts overlap naturally and the border forms into a curve.

Decorative finishes

Decorative finishes can add an extra dimension to painted or découpaged objects, and many have the effect of ageing an item. Here are some different finishes for you to try.

Distressed paint finish

The technique of distressing paint produces a soft, aged look and is particularly effective on a piece of furniture. Choose two colours of paint to go with your design or use just one colour over bare wood. The paint should be water-based emulsion. Here, pale blue is used under a cream top coat.

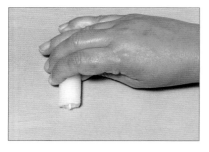
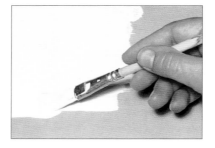
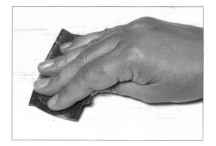

1. Paint the surface with the first colour and allow it to dry, or leave the wood bare. Rub candle wax over the surface, working with the grain. Pay particular attention to the areas that would distress naturally, such as handles or edges.

2. Brush a coat of the second colour over the wax. Brush in the direction of the grain. Allow to dry completely.

3. Rub the surface with a medium grade sandpaper. Again, work in the direction of the grain. The paint will rub off where there is wax underneath, leaving a distressed finish which can then be varnished or decorated with découpage.

This is a detail taken from the tray shown on page 19. The surface has been distressed, découpage has been applied, and the tray has then been crackled.

Crackling

There are many crackle varnishes available. They are all two-part varnishes and are applied one on top of the other. The bottom layer of varnish pulls the top layer apart to form cracks in the surface. I find that the most successful combination is an oil-based two-hour gold size as the first coat, and a water-based gum arabic solution as the second coat. As a general rule, a water-based product should not be applied over an oil-based product, but this is the exception to that rule.

1. Brush on a thin layer of two-hour gold size. Hold the article up to the light to check that the varnish is applied evenly and that it is covering the entire surface. Leave to dry in a cool, dry place for approximately one and a half hours, or until it is touch dry but still feels soft when pressed firmly with your finger.

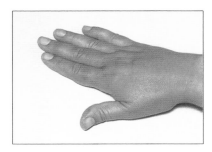

2. Brush on a coat of gum arabic solution. Use your hand to massage it into the bottom layer of varnish. Continue gently rubbing the surface for three to four minutes, or until the gum arabic begins to dry. Leave to dry naturally for at least two hours, but preferably overnight.

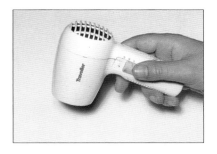

3. Use a hairdryer to gently heat the varnish for a couple of minutes. This process will cause the cracks to form, but at this stage they will barely show up.

4. Mix some artist's oil paint with a little white spirit until it is the consistency of toothpaste. Rub the thinned paint into the varnished surface using paper towelling.

5. Use a clean piece of paper towelling to wipe off all the excess paint, leaving colour only in the cracks. Leave to dry for about twelve hours. Seal with an oil- or spirit-based varnish.

Dutch metal gilding

Dutch metal leaf comes in three basic colours: gold, aluminium (silver) and copper (bronze). It can be bought as loose leaf or transfer leaf; the latter comes with a backing paper and is used in this example. The leaf adheres to water-based gold size. Once you have brushed on the size, the leaf must be applied within six hours.

> ### NOTE
>
> A coat of either red or black emulsion paint should be used underneath gold leaf. Blue works best underneath aluminium, and terracotta or green underneath copper.
>
> Metal leaf can be sealed with water- or spirit-based varnish. Shellac can also be used, but remember that this will alter the colour of the metal leaf.

1. Paint your item with a base coat of emulsion and allow to dry. Brush the size on to the areas you want to gild.

2. Leave to dry for at least five minutes, or until the size goes clear.

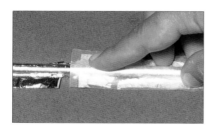

3. Cut the transfer leaf and backing paper into sizes suitable for your item. Carefully place each piece metal side down on to the clear size. Smooth over the backing paper with your fingers to transfer the leaf to the item. Gently peel away the backing paper. Repeat with the next piece of leaf, overlapping the first slightly. Continue until all the size is covered. Leave to dry for at least one hour.

4. Smooth over the metal leaf using a piece of cotton wool.

5. Brush off excess leaf using a soft paintbrush. Fill in any cracks using metallic paint, and use size and leftover leaf for any big holes. Seal with water- or spirit-based varnish.

> ### NOTE
>
> There are a number of metallic paints available which you can use as an alternative to Dutch metal leaf. The paints can be applied with a small paintbrush as shown opposite. Gold and silver felt-tip pens can also be used, but do try them out first on a piece of paper and make sure the various varnishes will not cause them to run or change colour.

A rich design of roses was applied on top of a distressed painted background to produce this classic bed tray. The tray was then given six layers of water-based varnish, before crackle varnish was applied. Burnt sienna oil paint was rubbed in to reveal the cracks. Three coats of oil-based polyurethane varnish were then applied, and the tray was finished with wax polish.

This collection of objects shows various decorative finishes, and all of the items use either Dutch metal leaf or metallic paint.

The oval trinket box was covered with Dutch metal gold leaf and then découpaged.

The green playing card box was distressed and then borders and a photocopy of a lion's head were colourwashed and stuck in place. Antique gold paint was then applied around the lid.

The table mat was découpaged and a border was then painted on with antique gold paint.

REPRODUCTION CHINESE LACQUERWORK

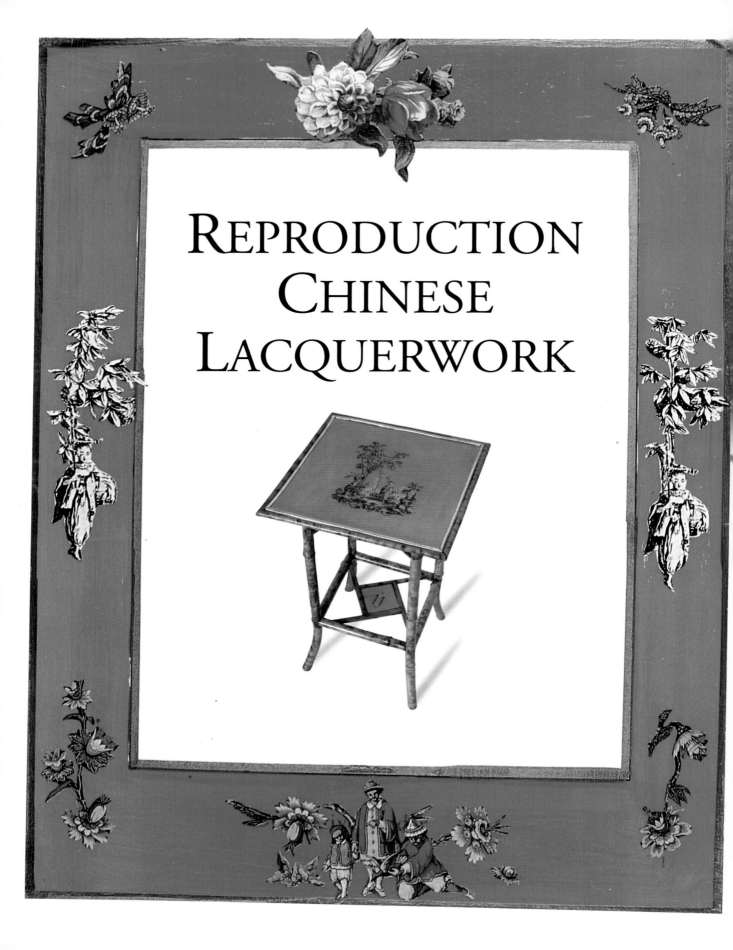

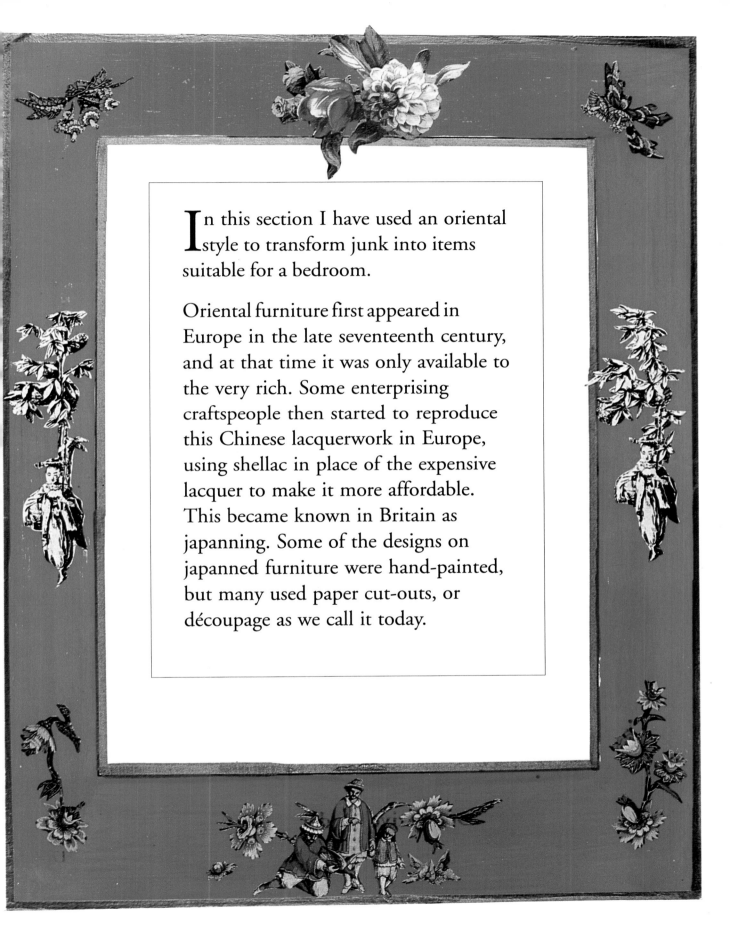

In this section I have used an oriental style to transform junk into items suitable for a bedroom.

Oriental furniture first appeared in Europe in the late seventeenth century, and at that time it was only available to the very rich. Some enterprising craftspeople then started to reproduce this Chinese lacquerwork in Europe, using shellac in place of the expensive lacquer to make it more affordable. This became known in Britain as japanning. Some of the designs on japanned furniture were hand-painted, but many used paper cut-outs, or découpage as we call it today.

This is the collection of junk before transformation. Turn to pages 26–29 to see how these items have been dramatically improved.

Bamboo table

A bamboo table was an ideal subject to transform using an oriental theme. I had intended to paint the legs to match the top, but having applied a coat of shellac as a primer, I then changed my mind as the bamboo looked lovely in its natural state. Spirit-based products, such as shellac, make ideal primers (particularly if you are unsure what the surface is underneath) as both oil and water-based products can be used over them.

YOU WILL NEED

Bamboo table

Sandpaper: medium grade

Wet-and-dry sandpaper: fine grade

Sandpaper block

Shellac

Emulsion paint: black and red

Water-based gold size

Four sheets of gold Dutch metal transfer leaf

PVA glue

Photocopies of a Chinese design

Watercolour paints

Small, sharp, pointed scissors

Chalk

Water-based varnish

Oil-based varnish

Beeswax polish

Duster

Four 2.5cm (1in) paintbrushes for emulsion paint and oil-based, water-based and spirit-based varnish.

No. 6 paintbrush for size and watercolour paints

Small glue brush

Sponge

Damp cloth

Small panel pins

Hammer

Wire wool: fine grade

1. Remove the beading from the table top. Sand down the table using a medium grade sandpaper. If the surface is very rough, begin with a coarse grade. Wrap the sandpaper around a sanding block to do large flat areas.

2. Remove any debris with a damp cloth. Allow to dry. Brush shellac over the entire table.

3. Paint the table top and bottom shelf with black emulsion. Allow to dry. Sand lightly with fine wet-and-dry sandpaper. Remove any debris with a damp cloth. Apply a coat of red emulsion. Leave to dry.

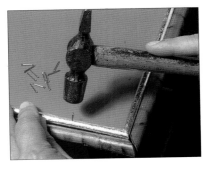

4. Apply gold leaf to the beading (see page 18). Use the No. 6 paintbrush to apply the size. Glue the beading back on to the table top using undiluted PVA glue. Tack the beading firmly in place using small panel pins.

5. Colour photocopied designs using watercolour paints and a No. 6 paintbrush. It does not matter if you go over some of the edges of the design. Leave to dry and then cut the images out (see page 12).

(see page 12)

NOTE

Paper stretches when it is wet, so any very small wrinkles that are left should disappear as the paper dries.

Do not worry about getting glue on the table. It will dry clear and will not show up when varnish is applied.

6. Arrange the images on the table top and the bottom shelf. When you are happy with the arrangement, mark the position of some of the points of the design with chalk.

7. Paste all over the back of the image with diluted PVA glue. Use the chalk marks as a guide to position the design back on the table top and bottom shelf.

8. Press out any wrinkles or air bubbles with a damp sponge and wipe away any remaining chalk marks. Leave to dry.

9. Paint the table top and bottom shelf with water-based varnish. Leave to dry and then repeat until you have built up six layers in total. Lightly sand with wet-and-dry sandpaper then remove any debris with a damp cloth. Allow to dry.

10. Paint the table top and bottom shelf with shellac. Allow to dry completely before applying a second coat. Repeat, building up the coats of shellac until you have the colour finish you like (this can be anything between two and ten coats). Leave to dry completely.

11. Sand the table top and bottom shelf with wet-and-dry sandpaper to remove any impurities from the surface. Remove any debris with a damp cloth. Apply a coat of oil-based varnish. Leave to dry overnight.

12. Apply wax polish to the table top, bottom shelf and legs using wire wool. Rub it in well.

13. Buff off the polish with a clean duster.

The finished bamboo table looks stunning alongside this matching table lamp.

The lamp base was gilded and then antiqued with shellac to enhance the colour of the gold. The lamp shade was then painted red, the edges were gilded and a final coat of water-based varnish was applied to complete the transformation.

The cut-out flowers on this sphere have all been stuck on to the inside of the glass. As the aperture is very small, a piece of damp cloth was tied to the end of a paintbrush to smooth the design into place. The inside was then painted with two shades of yellow paint to give a mottled look to the finished object.

This pretty jewellery box was a badly rusted tin before it was transformed. It was treated with a rust remover before being painted with red oxide primer and red emulsion paint. The flowers were stuck on and the whole box was then varnished in the same way as the table (see page 25).

This miniature papier-mâché trunk was given two coats of cream emulsion paint and then the features were picked out in pale blue. A willow pattern was applied and the surface was crackled to create a porcelain effect.

This impressive tray was created by first applying a coat of red oxide primer followed by a coat of black emulsion paint. The Chinese motif was applied to the centre and the edges were worked in antique gold paint. Water-based varnish was applied and then layers of oil-based polyurethane varnish were built up to provide a tough, heat-resistant finish.

27

This spectacular bed shows just how effective découpage can be, and how brilliantly it can transform an object. The headboard and footboard were sanded down and painted with two coats of black emulsion. The edges were then given a coat of red emulsion and gilded with gold Dutch metal transfer leaf. The découpage was added, then two coats of water-based varnish were applied. Eight coats of shellac were built up to deepen the colour and produce a rich effect. The bed was given two coats of oil-based varnish and finished off with wax polish.

This detail is taken from the inside of the footboard and shows the exquisite gift wrap used for this project. The large flower design looks very effective against the black background.

28

GEORGIAN
ELEGANCE

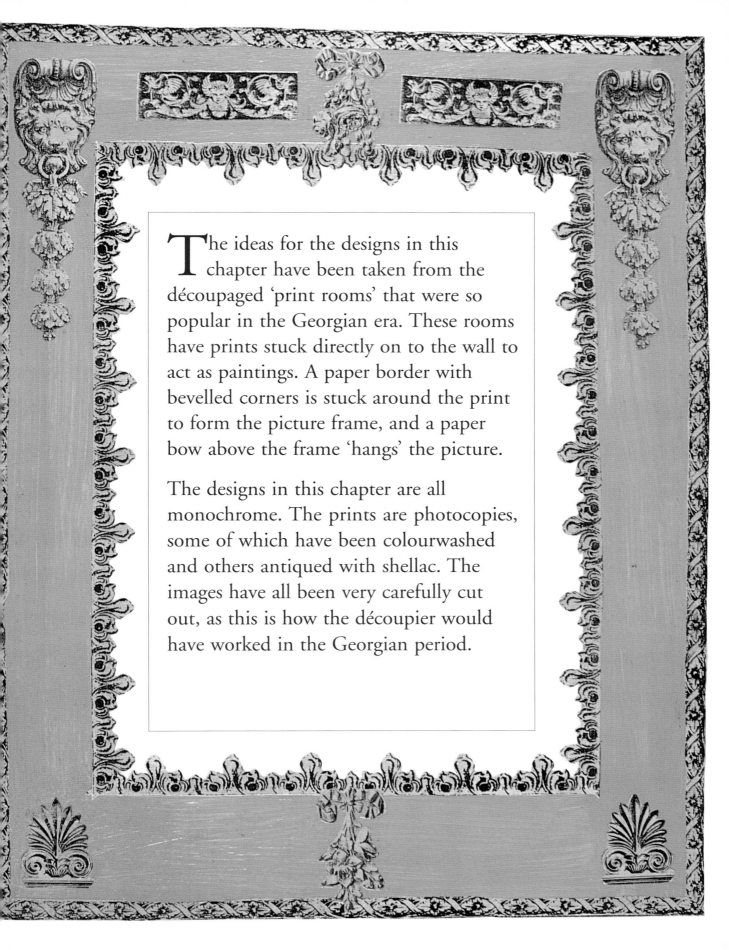

The ideas for the designs in this chapter have been taken from the découpaged 'print rooms' that were so popular in the Georgian era. These rooms have prints stuck directly on to the wall to act as paintings. A paper border with bevelled corners is stuck around the print to form the picture frame, and a paper bow above the frame 'hangs' the picture.

The designs in this chapter are all monochrome. The prints are photocopies, some of which have been colourwashed and others antiqued with shellac. The images have all been very carefully cut out, as this is how the découpier would have worked in the Georgian period.

*All the items in this collection of junk are well made, but tatty. They can
be dramatically transformed using gilding, crackling, distressing and
découpage techniques to create stunning new looks (see pages 34–37).*

China plate

I bought this plain white china plate because of its unusual shape. I thought that, when decorated, it would be useful to have on the hall table for keys. The method shown here for painting and découpaging the china plate can be used on any ceramics, including tiles.

YOU WILL NEED

- China plate
- Medium grade sandpaper
- PVA glue
- Emulsion paint: black
- Photocopied print and border design
- Water-based varnish
- Crackle varnish: two-hour gold size and gum arabic solution
- Hairdryer
- Artist's oil paint: burnt umber and cream
- Three 2.5cm (1in) paintbrushes for paint, water-based varnish and oil-based varnish
- Glue brush
- Sponge
- Paper towelling
- White spirit
- Damp cloth

1. Wash the plate in warm soapy water to remove any grease or dirt. Rub it down with a medium grade sandpaper to create a key. Remove any debris with a damp cloth.

2. Brush on a thin coat of diluted PVA glue and leave to dry.

3. Paint the plate with black emulsion. Leave to dry. Apply a second coat. Leave to dry.

4. Arrange the design and the border on the plate, and then glue it in place (see page 15). Leave the glue to dry. Apply a coat of water-based varnish.

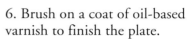

6. Brush on a coat of oil-based varnish to finish the plate.

5. Apply oil- and water-based crackle varnish to the plate (see page 17). Use cream oil paint to bring up the crackle on the black sections of the design, and dark brown to bring up the crackle on the white sections (see page 17).

The finished plate looks impressive, and can be used as a decorative or functional item. The final coat of oil-based varnish provides a protective finish, and the plate can be washed gently in warm soapy water. It must not, however, be put it in the dishwasher.

It is hard to believe that this plate is made of glass not gold! To create this illusion, a black and white antiqued design was applied to the underside of the plate, and it was then gilded. Water- then oil-based varnish were then applied over the gold metal leaf to make it durable. The finished plate can be washed gently in warm soapy water.

This mirror was in a poor state originally. The frame was cracked and had to be filled with wood filler, and the whole frame was rubbed down with medium grade sandpaper. It was then primed with sanding sealer, gilded with aluminium leaf and decorated with pale blue colourwashed prints. Finally, three coats of shellac were applied, giving the golden bronze colour.

The candlesticks were decorated using a black and white print coloured with French polish. The print was a photocopy of a piece of mock leopard skin fabric.

35

This little Italian-style trinket box has been given a new lease of life. The flower design was cut out very carefully and the intricate border was placed precisely. Crackle varnish was used to complete the transformation.

The work box, like the candlesticks on page 35, was decorated with a photocopy of a mock leopard skin fabric. The print was colourwashed to match the colour of the box. The elephants and border prints were also colourwashed before being glued on top of the leopard skin design. Eight coats of water-based varnish were then applied, and the box was polished.

OPPOSITE
This table looks dramatically different now. The transformation began by applying a pale blue undercoat. A cream top coat was painted on and it was then distressed. A black and white photocopied design was colourwashed cream and applied around the border and legs.

The magazine rack has a musical theme. The prints were coloured with French polish before being cut out and applied. Water-based varnish was then applied and the rack was finished with French polish.

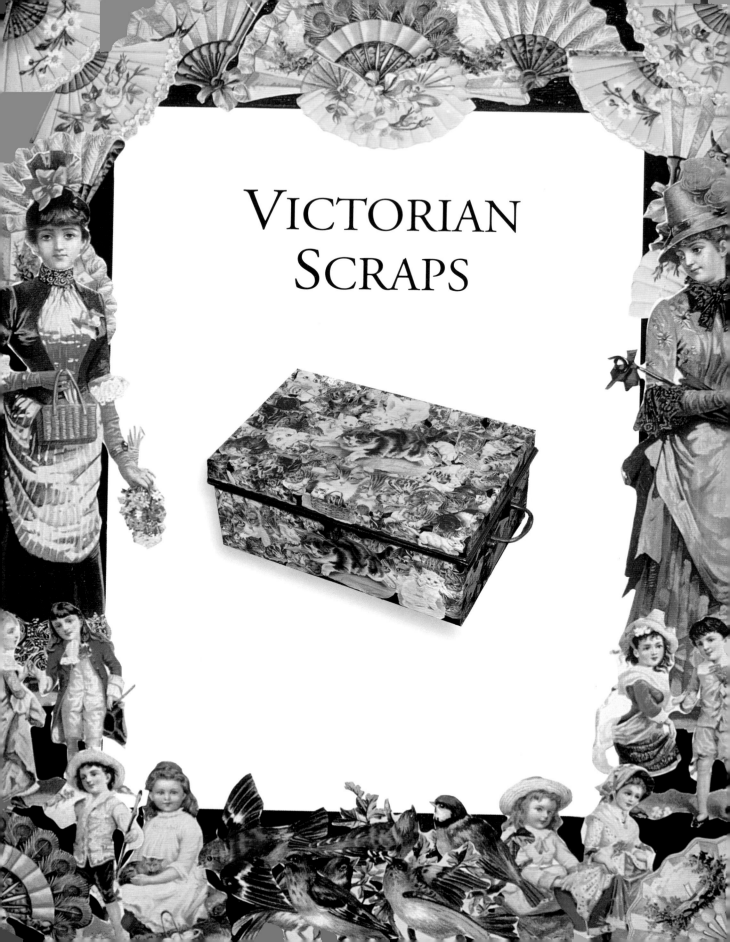

VICTORIAN
SCRAPS

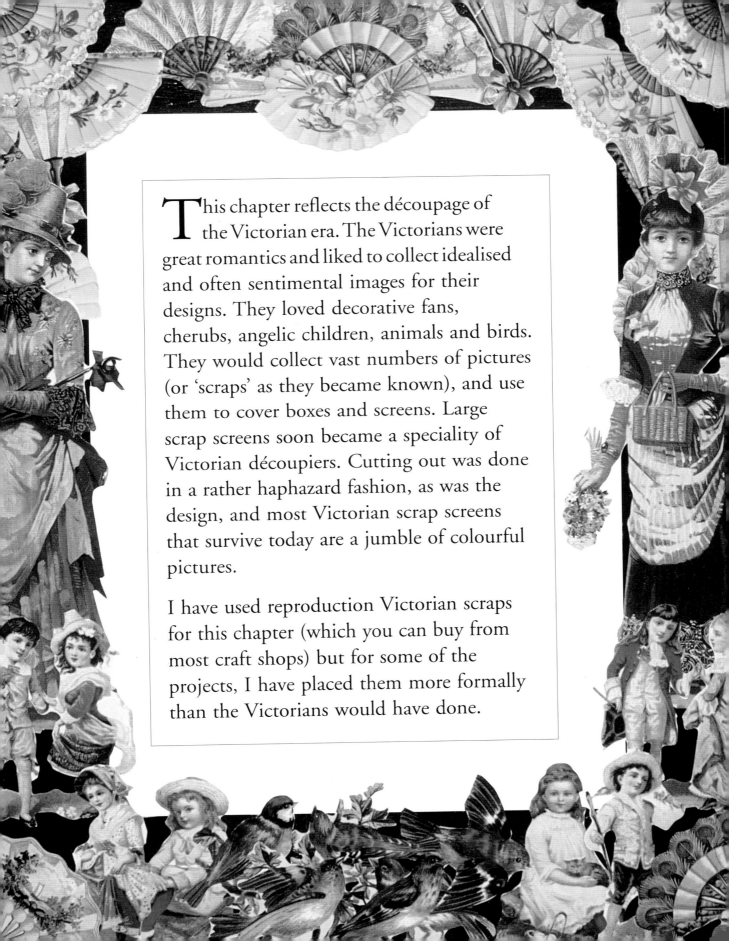

This chapter reflects the découpage of the Victorian era. The Victorians were great romantics and liked to collect idealised and often sentimental images for their designs. They loved decorative fans, cherubs, angelic children, animals and birds. They would collect vast numbers of pictures (or 'scraps' as they became known), and use them to cover boxes and screens. Large scrap screens soon became a speciality of Victorian découpiers. Cutting out was done in a rather haphazard fashion, as was the design, and most Victorian scrap screens that survive today are a jumble of colourful pictures.

I have used reproduction Victorian scraps for this chapter (which you can buy from most craft shops) but for some of the projects, I have placed them more formally than the Victorians would have done.

Here is the collection of junk before being transformed using the Victorian style of découpage. Turn to pages 42–45 to see how these items can be given striking face lifts.

Metal cash box

Metal is an easy material to découpage, and it is often very rewarding to work on as its transformation can be so startling. Metal trunks and boxes can be found in most junk shops. The old cash box featured in this project was in a good condition when I bought it, but do not be put off if you come across something that is rusted or dented. This need not matter as the rust can be removed easily with rust remover; and the dents, if not too big, can add to the appeal of the finished object, particularly if given an antique finish.

You will need

- Metal box
- Coarse grade sandpaper or wire wool
- Red oxide primer
- Emulsion paint: black
- Victorian scraps of cats
- PVA glue
- Water-based varnish
- Shellac
- Three 2.5cm (1in) paintbrushes for paint, water-based varnish and shellac
- Glue brush
- Damp cloth

1. Sand down the box using coarse grade sandpaper or wire wool. This will remove any rust or flaking paint and give the surface a key. If your box is badly rusted, use a rust remover first. Remove any debris with a damp cloth.

2. Paint the box with red oxide primer and leave to dry.

3. Apply a coat of black emulsion to the box. Leave to dry before applying a second coat. Again, leave to dry.

4. Paste cut-out cats on to the box using diluted PVA glue. Paint over the entire box with diluted PVA glue, making sure that all the edges are stuck down. Leave to dry completely.

Note

Try to cover the box completely, positioning the cats so that they face in all directions. I try to finish by placing one large cat on the centre of each surface to act as a focal point.

NOTE

Always allow the shellac to dry completely between coats to prevent a sticky mess accumulating.

Shellac is quite hard-wearing, but if your object is going to be used a lot, you could apply one or two coats of oil-based varnish on top of the shellac to give an even tougher protective finish.

5. Apply a coat of water-based varnish. Leave to dry before applying a second coat. Leave to dry.

6. Apply two or more coats of shellac, depending on how dark an antique finish you want (see page 25). Leave to dry thoroughly between coats.

This tin box looks splendid covered entirely with scraps, and is perfect for cat lovers! The box has a shelf inside, so it could be used on a large desk to store pens and paper.

Blanket boxes are always useful and can usually be found quite cheaply. This blanket box has been decorated using Victorian scraps arranged in a more formal style than the Victorians themselves would have worked. It was sanded down and painted with black emulsion paint. The edge of the lid and the feet were painted with antique gold paint and the design was then applied to the front and side panels and the top. It was varnished with eight layers of water-based varnish and finished off with two coats of oil-based varnish.

43

The round papier mâché box was découpaged and given a crackle finish to transform it into a lovely Victorian-style sewing box. The oil lamp was painted with red oxide primer and the Victorian scraps were applied directly on to this base. Coats of water-based followed by oil-based varnish were applied, making it suitable for use both indoors and outdoors.

A glass bowl has here been totally transformed. All the work has been done on the outside, which means that it can now be used as a decorative or functional item. The plain glass surface was crackled, and the varnish was sealed with clear-drying sanding sealer. The clowns were glued on, facing inwards. The bowl was then painted with green emulsion and gilded with copper Dutch metal leaf. Another set of clowns were stuck on, facing outwards. Water-based varnish was applied, followed by two coats of oil-based varnish. The finished bowl can be washed gently in warm soapy water.

This vase was treated in the same way as the plate featured on pages 33–34. The inside was painted and oil-based varnish was applied over water-based varnish, so the finished vase will hold water.

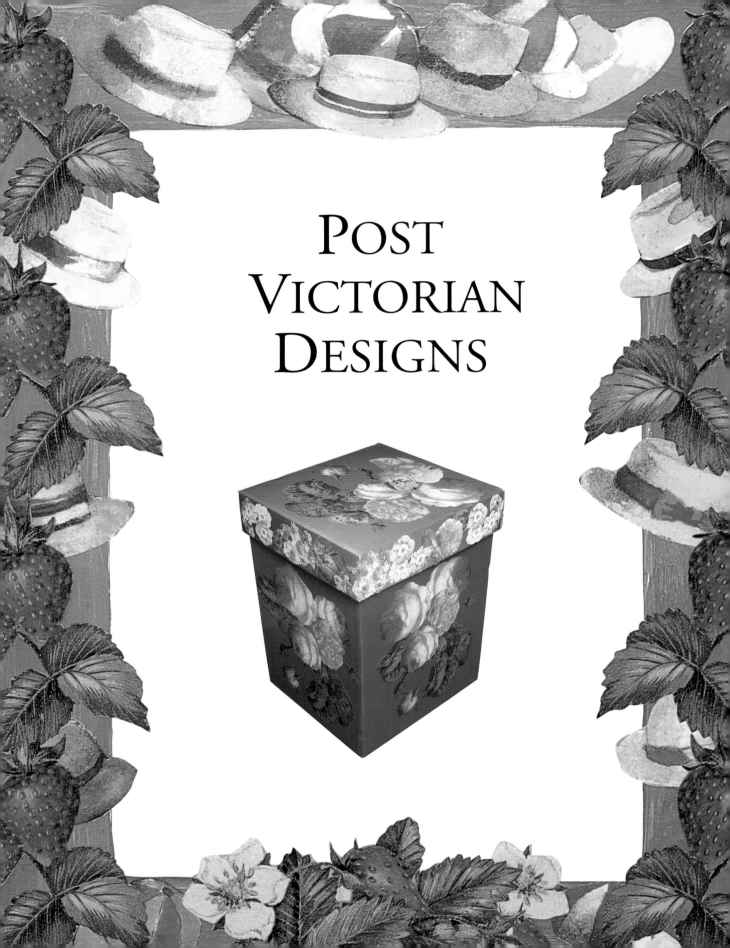

POST
VICTORIAN
DESIGNS

There is lots of wonderful gift wrap available today and it is partly because of this, that the art of découpage has become a popular pastime again. For this chapter, I have used some of my favourite papers which I have cut out carefully to produce wonderfully crisp images that look as if they have been painted on to the objects.

Some of the items featured in this chapter could be used in the garden; exterior oil-based varnishes are readily available, making this practical. The possibilities for découpaging are endless – all you need is imagination.

This disparate-looking collection of junk can be dramatically improved and turned into objects suitable for use in the conservatory and garden. Turn to pages 49-53 to see how effective this transformation can be.

Cardboard box

The cardboard box shown in this chapter was once the packaging for a Christmas present.
It was in good condition and so instead of painting it with water-based emulsion, I left it
as it was and decorated it using large, richly coloured roses.

YOU WILL NEED

Cardboard box
Flowery gift wrap
Small, sharp, pointed scissors
PVA glue
Water-based varnish
2.5cm (1in) paintbrush
Glue brush

1. Cut out the flowers from gift wrap, being careful to cut away all the islands of background (see page 12). Arrange your design on the box, making sure that the images on the sides will not be obscured when the lid is in place. Paste images on to all four sides of the box and the top of the lid using diluted PVA glue.

2. Glue smaller cut-out images around the side of the box lid to form a border. Make sure that the corner pieces are well stuck down to give a sharp edge. Leave to dry. Apply a coat of water-based varnish to the entire box. Leave to dry completely before applying a second coat.

The finished cardboard box can now be used as a very pretty storage container. Lots of packaging is suitable for decorating. Soaps, playing cards and many other items come in wonderful boxes, many of which cry out for a new look.

The kettle was treated in the same way as the cash box featured on pages 41–42 and will now make a wonderful watering can for indoor plants.

Terracotta flower pots can be turned into very decorative items. The pots at the front were sealed with PVA, one was painted with cream emulsion and the other left plain. The pots were then découpaged and given two coats of water-based varnish.

The ceramic pot at the back was treated in the same way as the plate on page 33.

The paraffin heater was treated with a rust remover and then sanded down. It was given a coat of red oxide primer, painted cream and the edges and detail were then picked out in green. It was decorated with strawberries and given four coats of water-based varnish to finish.

This pretty table was crackled and decorated with a wreath of flowers and butterflies. The butterflies were cut out very carefully, making sure that the antennae remained intact. The details on the legs were then picked out in green. The table was finished with water-based varnish followed by two coats of oil-based exterior varnish, making it weatherproof and therefore suitable for use in the garden.

OPPOSITE

This zinc bath was treated with a metal primer, painted with emulsion and then decorated with cut-out strawberries. It was then finished with four coats of water-based varnish, followed by two coats of oil-based exterior varnish, making it weatherproof. It could now be planted with flowers or even strawberries, or tubs of herbs could be placed in it.

Look out in your local junk shops for old zinc baths, watering cans and jugs. Make sure they do not leak if you want to use them, and remember to remove all rust before you apply a metal primer.

DEVELOPING
A THEME

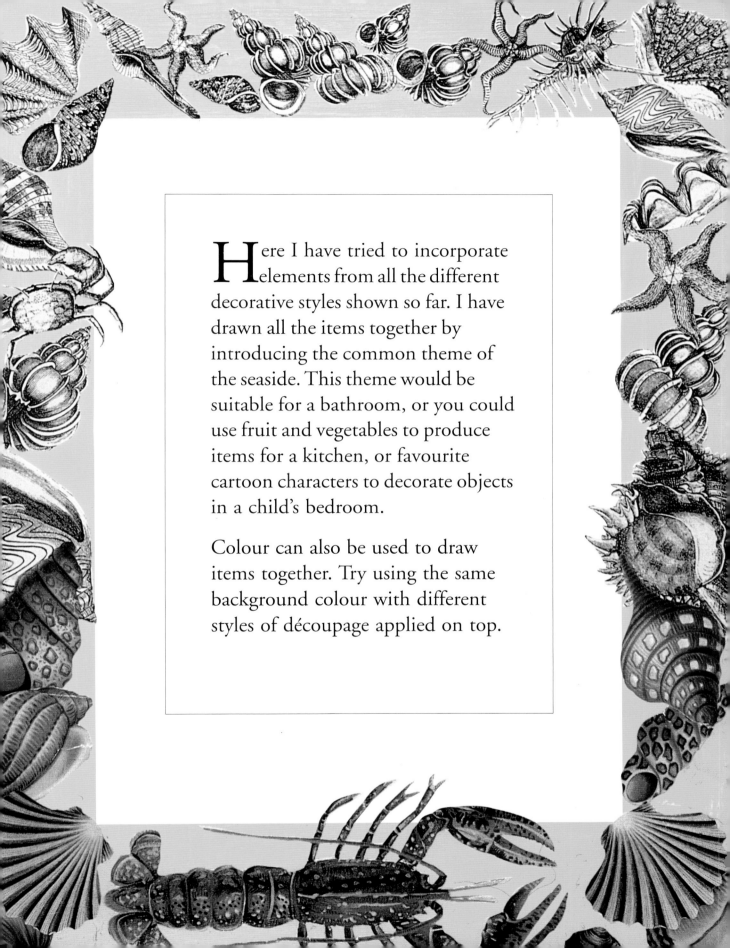

Here I have tried to incorporate elements from all the different decorative styles shown so far. I have drawn all the items together by introducing the common theme of the seaside. This theme would be suitable for a bathroom, or you could use fruit and vegetables to produce items for a kitchen, or favourite cartoon characters to decorate objects in a child's bedroom.

Colour can also be used to draw items together. Try using the same background colour with different styles of découpage applied on top.

Glass jar

The technique of decorating the inside of a glass object involves working in reverse: you apply the découpage first, then the paint. The inside of the jar is varnished, but the glass itself acts as the varnish for the outside. When choosing an item of glassware for this technique, make sure the gap at the top is big enough to get your hand into.
For this project, you can use a photocopier to alter the size of the images and thereby create small and large fish and shells.

YOU WILL NEED

Glass jar

Fish and shell photocopies in various sizes

Small, sharp, pointed scissors

PVA glue

Damp cloth

Water-based gold size

Dutch metal aluminium leaf

Metallic silver paint

Emulsion paint: yellow

Water-based varnish

Three 2.5cm (1in) paint-brushes for paint, water-based varnish and aluminium leaf (a soft, dry one should be used for the aluminium leaf)

Two 1cm ($\frac{1}{2}$in) paintbrushes for glue and size

No. 6 paintbrush for silver paint

1. Cut out the photocopied images (see page 12). Paste the right side of each image with diluted PVA glue and then stick them on to the inside of the glass jar. Gently wipe over the images with a damp cloth.

2. Paint the whole of the inside of the jar with diluted PVA glue. Check that all the edges are stuck down. Allow to dry.

NOTE

If you want to check your design before sticking, use some sticky plastic to stick your images on to the outside of the jar and transfer to the inside when gluing.

When sticking images on to glass, press out all the air bubbles with your fingers as they will show through the glass. Make sure all the edges are stuck down before wiping over the whole surface with a damp cloth.

OPPOSITE
This is the plain collection of junk before transformation. Turn to pages 58–61 to see how these items can be dramatically improved and made suitable for use in the bathroom.

3. Apply size carefully to the inside rim of the jar. Leave to dry for at least five minutes or until the size goes clear (see page 18).

4. Apply the aluminium transfer leaf to the clear size to cover the rim (see page 18). Leave to dry for at least two hours and then brush away the excess with a soft, dry brush.

5. Use a small paintbrush and silver paint to fill in any cracks on the rim. If there are any large holes, fill them in with size and any leftover aluminium leaf. Leave to dry.

6. Apply a coat of yellow emulsion to the inside of the jar. Leave to dry before applying a second coat. When that is dry, apply two coats of water-based varnish, again allowing time to dry between coats.

The finished jar looks splendid and is perfect for storing soap or cotton wool in the bathroom. The lid has been left plain, but you could choose to decorate it to match the jar.

The tiles on this page were originally all different colours. The orange tile on the right was left unpainted, but the others were decorated to match each other. Tiles can be treated in the same way as the china plate featured on pages 33–34. You can decorate tiles either on or off the wall, giving countless possibilities for redecorating. Before you begin, remember to wash the tiles in warm soapy water to remove any grease or soap. This is particularly important if you are decorating tiles on a wall in the kitchen or bathroom.

This chair has been decorated to create a very personal piece of découpage. It was first sanded down, then the details on the legs and back were painted with black emulsion. When dry, antique gold paint was applied. The rest of the chair was left unpainted so that it could be covered with photocopies of three generations of my family on seaside holidays. The Victorian style of placing pictures in all directions and almost one on top of the other was used. The chair was given a coat of water-based varnish, followed by four coasts of shellac to create a sepia look. Finally, three coats of oil-based varnish were applied. To create a black and white effect (see the Victorian hat box opposite), you can use water-based varnish in place of shellac.

This charming candle holder has been painted pale yellow and covered with colourwashed photocopies of coral. A coat of water-based varnish was then applied. It has not been crackled, but a little burnt umber artist's oil paint was rubbed into the corners to antique it. A layer of oil-based varnish was then applied.

This old Victorian hat box has been decorated with my family snaps in a Georgian style. Water-based varnish was used in place of shellac to ensure that the images remained black and white. Photographs can be used to great effect with découpage. You could use black and white or colour photocopies of wedding or christening photographs, for example, to create a very special commemorative piece. The service sheet and invitation could also be incorporated into the design.

This scoop was painted with a metal primer and blue emulsion paint. The colourful cut-out sea creatures were then glued on and five coats of water-based varnish were applied.

PUTTING WRONGS RIGHT

Everyone makes mistakes, however long they have been doing découpage. In fact, I have a house full of slight seconds that cannot be sold on to the trade! Most problems occur at the gluing stage, although using crackle varnish can also be problematic. Here are some of the more common mistakes and how to correct them.

Cutting away part of your design

This is easily rectified. Cut out all the elements of the design that you need and then at the gluing stage, simply fit them all together like a jigsaw puzzle. By the time you have finished varnishing, you will not see the joins.

Bubbles and bumps under the paper

If, once you have stuck on your design and allowed it to dry completely, you find bubbles of air trapped under the paper, cut though the bubble using a craft knife or scalpel. Try to get the cut working with an element in the design if possible. For instance, if the bubble is over a flower, cut along the line of a petal. Push a little PVA glue into the cut, then press down with your finger to push out the air and stick down the paper. The paper may overlap at the cut, which is why it is best to cut with the design if possible.

Some bumps may have glue rather than air in them. This occurs when the PVA glue mixture is too thick. Unfortunately, the problem cannot be rectified, but you should remember to dilute the PVA glue a little more when working on your next project.

Tearing the paper when gluing

When paper is wet with PVA glue, it tears easily. If you find that a particular paper is thin and tears easily, brush on a coat of sanding sealer to strengthen the paper. Leave to dry before cutting out.

Be careful when placing your design and do not rub the paper too hard when pushing out air bubbles. If the paper does tear, push it back together and glue it in place. If you find that there is a white edge to the tear once the glue has dried, use watercolour paints to mix up a colour that will match the design, then dab a little on to the tear. If the tear is big and you cannot push it back together, add a bit of extra design to cover it, such as a butterfly or a flower.

Breaking through the paper when sanding down the varnish

This will cause an unsightly white mark. Mix up a matching colour using watercolour paints. Dab the paint on to the white spot on the paper, then wipe it off with a piece of paper towelling. The watercolour paint will soak into the bare paper, but it will wipe away from the varnished areas. Allow the paint to dry, and then apply another coat of varnish. To prevent breaking the paper in future, do not attempt to sand until you have applied at least five coats of varnish.

Crackle varnish

Crackle varnish can be temperamental, particularly if used in extremes of heat, cold or humidity, so always try to apply crackle varnish in a moderate temperature.

If, after having shown up the cracks with artist's oil paint, there are one or two blotches that look unattractive, remove them with the corner of a piece of paper towelling dipped in a little white spirit. This will remove the oil paint and therefore hide the mistake. If, you are unhappy with the overall effect, remove all the oil paint using paper towelling soaked in white spirit. Seal the crackle varnish with sanding sealer then begin the crackling process again.

If the crackle varnish has wrinkles in it, this cannot be corrected. It is caused by the first coat of varnish being applied too thickly. Remember to apply it more thinly next time. If it has thickened in the jar, thin it by adding a small amount of white spirit.

Do not forget that crackle varnish must be sealed with a spirit- or oil-based varnish. Water-based products will remove the gum arabic solution and the cracks will therefore disappear as well.

Index